EMMANUEL JOSEPH

The Algorithm of Time, Exploring History's Lessons Through Technology and Thought

Copyright © 2025 by Emmanuel Joseph

All rights reserved. No part of this publication may be reproduced, stored or transmitted in any form or by any means, electronic, mechanical, photocopying, recording, scanning, or otherwise without written permission from the publisher. It is illegal to copy this book, post it to a website, or distribute it by any other means without permission.

First edition

This book was professionally typeset on Reedsy.
Find out more at reedsy.com

Contents

1	Chapter 1: The Genesis of Timekeeping	1
2	Chapter 2: The Enlightenment and the Birth of Modern Thought	3
3	Chapter 3: The Industrial Revolution: A Technological...	5
4	Chapter 4: The Digital Revolution: The Age of Information	7
5	Chapter 5: The Evolution of Education: From Oral Traditions...	9
6	Chapter 6: The Intersection of Technology and Healthcare	11
7	Chapter 7: The Impact of Transportation Technology on...	13
8	Chapter 8: The Role of Communication Technology in Shaping...	15
9	Chapter 9: The Intersection of Technology and Entertainment	17
10	Chapter 10: The Ethical Implications of Technological...	19
11	Chapter 11: The Role of Technology in Shaping Modern...	21
12	Chapter 12: The Impact of Technology on Environmental...	23
13	Chapter 13: The Role of Technology in Shaping Culture and...	25
14	Chapter 14: The Future of Work in a Technologically Driven...	27
15	Chapter 15: The Ethical Responsibility of Technological...	29

1

Chapter 1: The Genesis of Timekeeping

In ancient civilizations, the concept of timekeeping was integral to societal development. Early humans relied on natural phenomena like the movement of the sun and the phases of the moon to structure their lives. Sundials and water clocks emerged as the first technological advancements, allowing for a more precise measurement of time. These rudimentary tools laid the foundation for the complex systems we use today. The story of timekeeping is a testament to humanity's ingenuity and its relentless pursuit of order and understanding.

As societies grew more complex, so did their timekeeping methods. The invention of the mechanical clock in the Middle Ages revolutionized the way people perceived and managed time. These early clocks were marvels of engineering, showcasing the intricate interplay between gears, springs, and escapements. The mechanical clock not only synchronized communal activities but also reinforced the importance of punctuality and discipline in daily life. This period marked the beginning of a profound cultural shift, where time became a valuable and finite resource.

The Industrial Revolution brought about significant changes in timekeeping technology. The advent of the railroad and the telegraph necessitated the standardization of time across vast distances. Time zones were established, and the world became increasingly interconnected. The synchronization of time was crucial for coordinating economic activities, facilitating communication, and ensuring the efficient movement of goods and people. This era underscored the growing dependence on accurate timekeeping for the functioning of modern society.

Today, timekeeping has reached unprecedented levels of precision and accuracy. Atomic clocks, which measure time based on the vibrations of atoms, have redefined our understanding of time. These clocks are essential for various applications, including global positioning systems (GPS), telecommunications, and scientific research. The continuous advancements in timekeeping technology reflect our ongoing quest to master and manipulate time. As we delve deeper into the mysteries of time, we uncover new possibilities and challenges that shape our present and future.

2

Chapter 2: The Enlightenment and the Birth of Modern Thought

The Enlightenment, also known as the Age of Reason, was a pivotal period in human history that transformed our understanding of the world. This intellectual movement, which spanned the 17th and 18th centuries, emphasized reason, science, and individualism. Enlightenment thinkers such as John Locke, Voltaire, and Immanuel Kant challenged traditional beliefs and advocated for the application of scientific principles to all aspects of life. Their ideas laid the groundwork for modern philosophy, political theory, and social progress.

One of the key contributions of the Enlightenment was the development of the scientific method. This systematic approach to inquiry, championed by figures like Isaac Newton and René Descartes, revolutionized the way we acquire knowledge. By emphasizing observation, experimentation, and empirical evidence, the scientific method provided a reliable framework for understanding the natural world. This methodological shift not only advanced scientific discovery but also fostered a culture of critical thinking and skepticism.

The Enlightenment also had a profound impact on political thought and institutions. Enlightenment philosophers argued for the inherent rights of individuals and the importance of representative government. Their ideas influenced the drafting of foundational documents such as the United States Declaration of Independence and the French Declaration of the Rights of Man and of the Citizen. The principles of liberty, equality, and fraternity that emerged from this period continue to shape democratic societies and inspire movements for social justice.

The legacy of the Enlightenment extends beyond its immediate historical context. Its emphasis on reason, progress, and human potential remains a cornerstone of contemporary thought. The values and ideals that emerged during this period continue to inform debates on ethics, education, and governance. As we navigate the complexities of the modern world, the Enlightenment serves as a reminder of the power of rational inquiry and the enduring quest for knowledge and understanding.

3

Chapter 3: The Industrial Revolution: A Technological Transformation

The Industrial Revolution, which began in the late 18th century, marked a significant turning point in human history. This period of rapid industrialization and technological innovation fundamentally altered the way people lived and worked. The introduction of machinery and the establishment of factories transformed production processes, leading to increased efficiency and economic growth. The Industrial Revolution also brought about profound social changes, as urbanization and the rise of a new working class reshaped societal structures.

One of the key drivers of the Industrial Revolution was the development of new technologies. Innovations such as the steam engine, invented by James Watt, revolutionized transportation and manufacturing. The steam engine enabled the mass production of goods, facilitated the expansion of railways, and powered the growth of industries. Other technological advancements, including the spinning jenny and the power loom, revolutionized the textile industry and increased productivity. These innovations laid the foundation for the modern industrial economy.

The Industrial Revolution also had significant social and environmental impacts. The rapid growth of cities led to overcrowding, poor living conditions, and the exploitation of labor. Factory workers, including women and children, often faced long hours and hazardous working environments. The rise of industrial capitalism also widened the gap between the wealthy and the working class, leading to social tensions and calls for reform. The environmental consequences of industrialization, such as pollution and deforestation, also became increasingly apparent.

Despite its challenges, the Industrial Revolution brought about many positive changes. It led to the development of new infrastructure, such as roads, railways, and bridges, which facilitated the movement of goods and people. The increase in production and trade contributed to economic growth and improved living standards for many. The Industrial Revolution also spurred advancements in science and technology, paving the way for future innovations. The legacy of this transformative period continues to shape our modern world, highlighting the complex interplay between technology, society, and progress.

4

Chapter 4: The Digital Revolution: The Age of Information

The Digital Revolution, which began in the late 20th century, represents a profound shift in the way we access, process, and communicate information. This era of rapid technological advancement has fundamentally altered nearly every aspect of our lives. The development of digital technologies, such as computers, the internet, and mobile devices, has created a global interconnectedness that transcends geographical boundaries. The Digital Revolution has ushered in the age of information, transforming industries, economies, and societies.

One of the most significant aspects of the Digital Revolution is the proliferation of the internet. The internet has revolutionized communication, enabling instant access to information and facilitating global connectivity. Social media platforms, email, and messaging apps have transformed the way we interact with one another, breaking down barriers and creating new opportunities for collaboration. The internet has also democratized access to knowledge, empowering individuals with the ability to learn, share, and create.

The impact of digital technologies extends beyond communication. The rise of big data and artificial intelligence (AI) has revolutionized industries such as healthcare, finance, and transportation. Big data analytics allows for the processing and analysis of vast amounts of information, leading to more informed decision-making and improved efficiency. AI technologies, such as machine learning and natural language processing, are transforming the way we work and live, from personalized healthcare to autonomous vehicles. The Digital Revolution is driving innovation and shaping the future of our world.

However, the Digital Revolution also presents challenges and ethical considerations. The digital divide, which refers to the gap between those with access to digital technologies and those without, highlights disparities in opportunities and resources. Privacy concerns and the ethical use of data are also critical issues in the digital age. As we continue to navigate the complexities of the Digital Revolution, it is essential to address these challenges and ensure that the benefits of digital technologies are accessible to all.

5

Chapter 5: The Evolution of Education: From Oral Traditions to E-Learning

Education has undergone a profound transformation throughout history, reflecting the changing needs and values of societies. In ancient times, education was primarily oral, with knowledge passed down through storytelling and oral traditions. These early forms of education were deeply rooted in culture and community, fostering a sense of identity and continuity. As societies became more complex, the need for formal education systems emerged, leading to the establishment of schools and universities.

The advent of the printing press in the 15th century revolutionized education by making written knowledge more accessible. The mass production of books enabled the spread of ideas and information, democratizing access to education. The printing press also facilitated the development of standardized curricula and the dissemination of scientific knowledge. This period marked a significant shift in the way people learned, as written texts became the primary medium for education.

The 20th century brought about further changes in education with the rise of compulsory schooling and the expansion of higher education. Governments recognized the importance of education for social and economic development, leading to the establishment of public education systems. The focus on universal education aimed to provide equal opportunities for all individuals, regardless of their background. The 20th century also saw the development of new teaching methods and educational theories, emphasizing the importance of critical thinking, creativity, and lifelong learning.

In the digital age, education is undergoing yet another transformation with the advent of e-learning and online education. Digital technologies have made education more accessible and flexible, allowing individuals to learn at their own pace and from anywhere in the world. Online courses, virtual classrooms, and educational apps are revolutionizing the way we learn, breaking down traditional barriers and creating new opportunities for personal and professional growth. As we move forward, the evolution of education will continue to be shaped by technological advancements and the changing needs of society.

6

Chapter 6: The Intersection of Technology and Healthcare

The field of healthcare has been profoundly transformed by technological advancements, leading to improved patient outcomes and enhanced quality of life. From the development of vaccines and antibiotics to the advent of medical imaging and robotic surgery, technology has played a critical role in advancing medical knowledge and practice. The intersection of technology and healthcare has revolutionized diagnosis, treatment, and prevention, making healthcare more efficient, accurate, and accessible.

One of the most significant technological advancements in healthcare is the development of medical imaging techniques. Technologies such as X-rays, MRI, and CT scans have revolutionized the way we diagnose and treat

continue

One of the most significant technological advancements in healthcare is the development of medical imaging techniques. Technologies such as X-rays, MRI, and CT scans have revolutionized the way we diagnose and treat medical conditions. These imaging techniques provide detailed insights into the human body, allowing for early detection and accurate diagnosis of diseases. They have also enabled minimally invasive procedures, reducing recovery times and improving patient outcomes. Medical imaging continues to evolve, with innovations such as 3D imaging and advanced image processing techniques pushing the boundaries of what is possible.

Another major technological breakthrough in healthcare is the development of electronic health records (EHRs). EHRs have streamlined the management of patient information, making it easier for healthcare providers to access and share medical data. This has led to more coordinated and efficient care, reducing the risk of medical errors and improving patient safety. EHRs also facilitate data-driven decision-making, enabling healthcare providers to analyze patient data and identify trends and patterns that can inform treatment plans and public health strategies.

Telemedicine is another transformative technology that has gained prominence in recent years. Telemedicine leverages digital communication tools to provide remote healthcare services, making it possible for patients to consult with healthcare providers from the comfort of their homes. This has been particularly valuable in rural and underserved areas, where access to healthcare services may be limited. Telemedicine has also proven to be a critical tool during public health emergencies, such as the COVID-19 pandemic, enabling continuity of care while minimizing the risk of infection.

The integration of artificial intelligence (AI) in healthcare is driving innovation and improving patient outcomes. AI algorithms can analyze vast amounts of medical data, assisting in the early detection and diagnosis of diseases. Machine learning models can predict patient outcomes and identify high-risk patients, enabling personalized treatment plans and proactive interventions. AI-powered tools, such as chatbots and virtual assistants, are also enhancing patient engagement and improving the efficiency of administrative tasks. As AI technology continues to advance, its potential to transform healthcare is vast and promising.

7

Chapter 7: The Impact of Transportation Technology on Society

Transportation technology has played a crucial role in shaping human civilization and driving economic development. From the invention of the wheel to the development of modern aviation, advancements in transportation have revolutionized the way we move goods and people. These technological innovations have not only facilitated trade and commerce but have also transformed the social, cultural, and environmental landscape of our world.

One of the earliest and most significant transportation innovations was the invention of the wheel. The wheel enabled the development of carts and wagons, making it easier to transport goods over long distances. This innovation facilitated trade and commerce, connecting different regions and cultures. The development of roads and bridges further improved transportation infrastructure, enabling the efficient movement of goods and people. The wheel remains a fundamental technology that continues to underpin modern transportation systems.

The Industrial Revolution brought about significant advancements in transportation technology. The development of the steam engine revolutionized transportation, leading to the rise of railways and steamships. Railways facilitated the rapid movement of goods and people, connecting cities and regions and driving economic growth. Steamships enabled global trade, connecting distant continents and cultures. The Industrial Revolution marked a period of unprecedented mobility and connectivity, transforming the social and economic fabric of society.

The 20th century saw the rise of the automobile and the development of modern aviation. The invention of the internal combustion engine and the mass production of automobiles revolutionized personal transportation, making it accessible to the masses. The construction of highways and the expansion of road networks facilitated the growth of suburbs and changed the way people lived and worked. The development of commercial aviation made it possible to travel long distances in a short amount of time, shrinking the world and enabling global travel and trade.

Today, transportation technology continues to evolve, with innovations such as electric vehicles, high-speed trains, and autonomous vehicles pushing the boundaries of what is possible. These advancements hold the promise of reducing carbon emissions, improving safety, and enhancing the efficiency of transportation systems. As we look to the future, the continued development of transportation technology will play a critical role in shaping our world and addressing the challenges of urbanization, climate change, and sustainable development.

8

Chapter 8: The Role of Communication Technology in Shaping Human Interaction

Communication technology has profoundly influenced the way we connect, share information, and interact with one another. From the invention of the telegraph to the rise of social media, advancements in communication technology have transformed the social and cultural landscape of our world. These innovations have enabled real-time communication across vast distances, fostering global connectivity and collaboration.

The invention of the telegraph in the 19th century marked a significant milestone in communication technology. The telegraph allowed for the rapid transmission of messages over long distances, revolutionizing the way information was exchanged. This innovation facilitated international trade, diplomacy, and journalism, connecting people and cultures like never before. The telegraph laid the foundation for subsequent advancements in communication technology, including the telephone and radio.

The 20th century witnessed the rise of mass communication technologies, such as television and the internet. Television brought visual storytelling into people's homes, shaping public opinion and culture. The internet revolutionized communication by enabling instant access to information and facilitating global connectivity. Email, instant messaging, and social media platforms transformed the way we interact with one another, breaking down geographical barriers and creating new opportunities for collaboration and engagement.

Social media has had a profound impact on human interaction, transforming the way we communicate and share information. Platforms such as Facebook, Twitter, and Instagram have created virtual communities where people can connect, share experiences, and engage in discussions. Social media has also given rise to new forms of expression and activism, enabling individuals to amplify their voices and advocate for social change. However, the rise of social media has also raised concerns about privacy, misinformation, and the impact on mental health.

The future of communication technology holds exciting possibilities, with innovations such as virtual reality (VR) and augmented reality (AR) poised to transform the way we interact and experience the world. These technologies have the potential to create immersive and interactive communication experiences, bridging the gap between physical and digital spaces. As communication technology continues to evolve, it will play a crucial role in shaping human interaction, fostering global connectivity, and addressing the challenges of the digital age.

9

Chapter 9: The Intersection of Technology and Entertainment

The entertainment industry has been profoundly influenced by technological advancements, leading to the creation of new forms of media and transforming the way we consume and engage with content. From the invention of the phonograph to the rise of streaming services, technology has revolutionized the entertainment landscape, making it more accessible, diverse, and interactive.

The invention of the phonograph in the late 19th century marked a significant milestone in the history of entertainment. The phonograph allowed for the recording and playback of sound, revolutionizing the way people experienced music. This innovation paved the way for the development of the music industry, enabling the mass production and distribution of recorded music. The phonograph also laid the foundation for subsequent advancements in audio technology, including the development of radio and recorded soundtracks for film.

The 20th century saw significant advancements in film and television technology. The introduction of synchronized sound, color film, and special effects transformed the cinematic experience, making it more immersive and engaging. Television brought visual storytelling into people's homes, creating a shared cultural experience and shaping public opinion. The development of home video technology, such as VHS and DVD, further revolutionized the way people consumed entertainment, allowing for the recording and playback of content on-demand.

The digital age has brought about a new era of entertainment with the rise of the internet and streaming services. Platforms such as Netflix, YouTube, and Spotify have transformed the way we access and consume content, making it more convenient and personalized. Streaming services have also democratized content creation, allowing independent artists and creators to reach global audiences. The rise of social media has further amplified the reach of entertainment, enabling fans to connect with their favorite artists and participate in online communities.

The future of entertainment technology holds exciting possibilities, with innovations such as virtual reality (VR), augmented reality (AR), and interactive storytelling poised to transform the way we experience content. These technologies have the potential to create immersive and interactive entertainment experiences, blurring the lines between the physical and digital worlds. As technology continues to evolve, it will shape the future of entertainment, creating new opportunities for creativity, engagement, and connection.

10

Chapter 10: The Ethical Implications of Technological Advancements

Technological advancements have brought about numerous benefits and opportunities, but they also raise important ethical considerations. As we continue to innovate and develop new technologies, it is essential to carefully consider their impact on society, the environment, and individual rights. The ethical implications of technological advancements are complex and multifaceted, requiring thoughtful reflection and responsible decision-making.

One of the key ethical considerations in technology is the issue of privacy. The rise of digital technologies, such as the internet, social media, and big data, has led to the collection and storage of vast amounts of personal information. While these technologies offer numerous benefits, such as personalized services and improved decision-making, they also raise concerns about data privacy and security. Ensuring that individuals have control over their personal information and that it is used responsibly is a critical ethical challenge in the digital age.

Another important ethical consideration is the impact of technology on employment and the workforce. Technological advancements, such as automation and artificial intelligence, have the potential to improve efficiency and productivity, but they also raise concerns about job displacement and economic inequality. As certain tasks become automated, there is a risk that workers may be displaced from their jobs, leading to unemployment and social instability. Addressing the ethical implications of automation requires a thoughtful approach to workforce development, education, and social safety nets.

Environmental sustainability is another critical ethical consideration in technology. The development and use of certain technologies can have significant environmental impacts, such as pollution, resource depletion, and climate change. Ensuring that technological advancements are environmentally sustainable and that they contribute to the well-being of the planet is a key ethical challenge. This requires a commitment to sustainable practices, responsible resource management, and the development of green technologies.

The ethical implications of technological advancements are also evident in the development and use of artificial intelligence (AI). AI technologies, such as machine learning and facial recognition, have the potential to improve efficiency, accuracy, and decision-making. However, they also raise important ethical questions about bias, accountability, and transparency. Ensuring that AI systems are designed and implemented in a fair and ethical manner is crucial for minimizing potential harms and maximizing benefits. This requires ongoing dialogue and collaboration among stakeholders, including technologists, policymakers, and the public.

11

Chapter 11: The Role of Technology in Shaping Modern Economics

The influence of technology on modern economics cannot be overstated. Technological advancements have driven economic growth, transformed industries, and reshaped the labor market. From the rise of digital currencies to the development of the gig economy, technology has created new opportunities and challenges for businesses, workers, and policymakers.

One of the most significant technological developments in modern economics is the rise of digital currencies, such as Bitcoin and other cryptocurrencies. Digital currencies leverage blockchain technology to facilitate secure and decentralized transactions. These innovations have the potential to disrupt traditional financial systems, offering new opportunities for financial inclusion and reducing the reliance on intermediaries. However, digital currencies also raise important questions about regulation, security, and the potential for misuse.

The development of the gig economy is another example of how technology is reshaping the labor market. Digital platforms, such as Uber, Airbnb, and TaskRabbit, have created new opportunities for flexible and on-demand work. The gig economy offers individuals the ability to work independently, set their own schedules, and earn income from a variety of sources. However, it also raises concerns about job security, worker rights, and the classification of gig workers. Ensuring that the gig economy operates in a fair and equitable manner is a key challenge for policymakers and businesses.

E-commerce has also been profoundly impacted by technology. The rise of online marketplaces, such as Amazon and Alibaba, has transformed the way consumers shop and businesses operate. E-commerce platforms offer convenience, a wide selection of products, and competitive pricing, driving significant changes in retail and supply chain management. The growth of e-commerce has also led to the development of new technologies, such as automated warehouses and last-mile delivery solutions, further enhancing efficiency and customer experience.

The integration of technology in finance, known as fintech, is driving innovation and improving access to financial services. Fintech solutions, such as mobile banking, peer-to-peer lending, and robo-advisors, are making financial services more accessible and affordable. These technologies have the potential to empower individuals and small businesses, providing them with the tools and resources needed to manage their finances effectively. As technology continues to advance, it will play a critical role in shaping the future of modern economics and addressing the challenges of financial inclusion and economic inequality.

12

Chapter 12: The Impact of Technology on Environmental Sustainability

Technology has a significant impact on environmental sustainability, offering both opportunities and challenges. While certain technological advancements have contributed to environmental degradation, others hold the potential to mitigate these impacts and promote sustainable development. The role of technology in addressing environmental challenges is complex and multifaceted, requiring a balanced and thoughtful approach.

One of the key areas where technology can contribute to environmental sustainability is in the development of renewable energy sources. Technologies such as solar, wind, and hydroelectric power offer cleaner alternatives to fossil fuels, reducing greenhouse gas emissions and dependence on non-renewable resources. Advancements in energy storage and grid management are also improving the efficiency and reliability of renewable energy systems. The transition to renewable energy is a critical component of global efforts to combat climate change and promote sustainable development.

Energy efficiency is another important aspect of environmental sustainability. Technological innovations, such as smart grids, energy-efficient appliances, and green building materials, can significantly reduce energy consumption and environmental impact. Smart grids use digital technology to optimize the distribution and consumption of electricity, reducing waste and improving reliability. Energy-efficient appliances and green building materials reduce the environmental footprint of households and businesses, contributing to overall sustainability efforts.

Sustainable agriculture is another area where technology can make a significant difference. Precision agriculture, which leverages digital tools and data analytics, allows farmers to optimize resource use and increase crop yields. Technologies such as drones, sensors, and satellite imagery provide valuable insights into soil health, weather patterns, and crop conditions, enabling more informed decision-making. Sustainable agriculture practices, supported by technology, can help address food security challenges and reduce the environmental impact of farming.

However, the development and use of technology also present environmental challenges. The production and disposal of electronic devices, for example, contribute to e-waste and resource depletion. The extraction of raw materials for technology manufacturing can lead to habitat destruction and pollution. Addressing these challenges requires a commitment to sustainable practices, such as recycling, responsible sourcing, and the development of green technologies. As we continue to innovate and develop new technologies, it is essential to consider their environmental impact and strive for a balance between progress and sustainability.

13

Chapter 13: The Role of Technology in Shaping Culture and Identity

Technology has a profound influence on culture and identity, shaping the way we express ourselves, connect with others, and understand the world around us. From the rise of digital art to the proliferation of social media, technological advancements have transformed cultural practices and created new opportunities for creativity and self-expression. The interplay between technology, culture, and identity is complex and dynamic, reflecting the diverse ways in which individuals and communities engage with technology.

Digital art is one of the most significant ways in which technology has influenced cultural expression. Digital tools and platforms have democratized the creation and dissemination of art, allowing artists to experiment with new forms and reach global audiences. Digital art encompasses a wide range of practices, including digital painting, 3D modeling, animation, and interactive installations. These innovations have expanded the possibilities of artistic expression and challenged traditional notions of what constitutes art.

Social media has also had a profound impact on culture and identity, transforming the way we communicate and share experiences. Platforms such as Instagram, TikTok, and Twitter provide individuals with the tools to curate their online personas and connect with others who share similar interests. Social media has given rise to new forms of cultural expression, such as memes, viral videos, and influencer marketing. It has also created virtual communities where individuals can find support, share knowledge, and engage in cultural exchange.

The rise of digital media has also influenced the way we consume and engage with cultural content. Streaming services, such as Netflix, Spotify, and YouTube, have made it easier than ever to access a diverse range of music, films, and television shows. This accessibility has contributed to the globalization of culture, allowing individuals to explore and appreciate different cultural practices and perspectives. Digital media has also given rise to new forms of storytelling, such as interactive narratives and virtual reality experiences, pushing the boundaries of traditional media.

However, the influence of technology on culture and identity also raises important questions about authenticity, representation, and the digital divide. The curation of online personas can lead to questions about the authenticity of self-expression, and the prevalence of digital media can contribute to the homogenization of culture. Ensuring that diverse voices and perspectives are represented in digital spaces is a critical challenge. Addressing the digital divide, which refers to the disparities in access to technology and digital resources, is also essential for ensuring that the benefits of technological advancements are accessible to all.

14

Chapter 14: The Future of Work in a Technologically Driven World

The future of work is being shaped by rapid technological advancements, driving significant changes in the labor market, job roles, and work practices. From automation and artificial intelligence to remote work and digital platforms, technology is transforming the way we work and creating new opportunities and challenges for businesses and workers. Understanding and navigating the future of work requires a proactive and adaptive approach.

One of the most significant trends shaping the future of work is the rise of automation and artificial intelligence (AI). Automation technologies, such as robotics and machine learning, have the potential to improve efficiency and productivity by performing repetitive and routine tasks. AI technologies, such as natural language processing and predictive analytics, can enhance decision-making and provide valuable insights. While these technologies offer numerous benefits, they also raise concerns about job displacement and the need for reskilling and upskilling the workforce.

Remote work is another important trend that has been accelerated by advancements in digital communication tools and the COVID-19 pandemic. Remote work offers flexibility and convenience, allowing individuals to work from anywhere with an internet connection. Digital tools, such as video conferencing, collaboration platforms, and cloud computing, have enabled seamless remote work and virtual collaboration. However, remote work also presents challenges, such as maintaining work-life balance, fostering team cohesion, and ensuring cybersecurity.

The rise of digital platforms is reshaping the way work is organized and delivered. Platforms such as freelancing websites, gig economy apps, and online marketplaces provide individuals with new opportunities for independent work and entrepreneurship. These platforms offer flexibility and access to a global market, but they also raise questions about worker rights, job security, and the classification of platform workers. Ensuring that digital platform work operates in a fair and equitable manner is a key challenge for businesses and policymakers.

As we look to the future, it is essential to prepare for the changes and opportunities brought about by technological advancements. This requires a focus on education and training, ensuring that individuals have the skills needed to thrive in a technologically driven world. Lifelong learning, reskilling, and upskilling will be critical for adapting to new job roles and work practices. Policymakers, businesses, and workers must collaborate to create a future of work that is inclusive, equitable, and sustainable.

15

Chapter 15: The Ethical Responsibility of Technological Innovation

As we continue to innovate and develop new technologies, it is essential to recognize the ethical responsibility that comes with technological advancement. The decisions we make about technology have far-reaching implications for society, the environment, and future generations. Ensuring that technological innovation is guided by ethical principles and values is crucial for creating a just and sustainable future.

One of the key ethical responsibilities in technological innovation is ensuring that technology is used for the benefit of all humanity. This means developing technologies that promote social good, improve quality of life, and address pressing global challenges. It also involves considering the potential unintended consequences of technology and taking steps to mitigate any negative impacts. Ethical innovation requires a commitment to transparency, accountability, and inclusivity, ensuring that all voices are heard and considered in the development process.

Another important ethical consideration is the principle of justice and fairness. This involves ensuring that the benefits and burdens of technological advancements are distributed equitably across society. It means addressing issues such as the digital divide, where certain populations may lack access to technology and its benefits. It also involves considering the impact of technology on marginalized and vulnerable communities, ensuring that they are not disproportionately affected by negative outcomes. Ethical innovation requires a commitment to social justice and the equitable distribution of resources and opportunities.

Environmental sustainability is also a critical ethical responsibility in technological innovation. As we develop new technologies, it is essential to consider their environmental impact and strive for sustainable practices. This involves minimizing resource consumption, reducing waste, and promoting the use of renewable energy sources. It also means developing technologies that can address environmental challenges, such as climate change, pollution, and resource depletion. Ethical innovation requires a commitment to environmental stewardship and the protection of our planet for future generations.

Finally, ethical technological innovation involves a commitment to human rights and dignity. This means ensuring that technology is developed and used in a way that respects and protects individual rights and freedoms. It involves addressing issues such as privacy, data security, and surveillance, ensuring that individuals have control over their personal information and are protected from harm. Ethical innovation also means considering the impact of technology on human well-being, ensuring that it enhances rather than diminishes quality of life.

As we continue to innovate and develop new technologies, it is essential to prioritize ethical considerations and ensure that our advancements contribute to a just, equitable, and sustainable future. By embracing ethical principles and values, we can harness the power of technology to create a better world for all.

he Algorithm of Time: Exploring History's Lessons Through Technology and Thought

Ever wondered how the ticking of a clock has shaped the world? "The Algorithm of Time: Exploring History's Lessons Through Technology and Thought" delves into the fascinating journey of timekeeping and technology, unraveling how these advances have steered human progress. From the

CHAPTER 15: THE ETHICAL RESPONSIBILITY OF TECHNOLOGICAL...

invention of the sundial to the rise of the digital age, each chapter explores pivotal moments where innovation and thought converged to transform society.

Discover how the Enlightenment sparked a revolution in reason and science, leading to modern philosophies that continue to influence our lives. Journey through the Industrial Revolution, where steam engines and machinery altered the landscape of work and society. Explore the Digital Revolution, the dawn of the internet, and how it has reshaped our interactions and the global economy.

This book also addresses the ethical dimensions of technological advancement, considering the responsibilities we bear as creators and users of new technologies. It shines a light on the impact of technology on education, healthcare, transportation, and entertainment, reflecting on the cultural and environmental implications of our rapidly changing world.

"The Algorithm of Time" is a compelling narrative that weaves together historical insights and technological milestones, offering a thoughtful perspective on how we can harness the lessons of the past to create a better future. It is an essential read for anyone curious about the interplay between innovation, society, and ethics.

www.ingramcontent.com/pod-product-compliance
Lightning Source LLC
LaVergne TN
LVHW020502080526
838202LV00057B/6115